CW00726521

Ha   Hor   Ho   H

Har   Ho   Hee   He

Har   H

Ha   Ho

Canadian representatives: General Publishing Co., Ltd., 30 Lesmill Road,
Don Mills, Ontario M3B 2T6.

Library of Congress Cataloging-in-Publication Number 93-87402

ISBN 1-56138-421-6

This book may be ordered by mail from the publisher.
Please add $1.00 for postage and handling.
But try your bookstore first!

Running Press Book Publishers
125 South Twenty-second Street
Philadelphia, Pennsylvania 19103-4399

the big book of

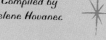
Riddles

Compiled by
Helene Hovanec

Running Press
Philadelphia • London

Introduction

Riddles appeal to the child in all of us. There's something about a simple question with a corny answer that makes us groan first and then giggle. And groaning and giggling are good for children and adults alike!

Of course, there's a logic to some riddles—like the

one Oedipus solved for the Sphinx: "What walks on four legs in the morning, two legs in the afternoon, and three legs in the evening?" His correct answer— "Man, who crawls as a child, walks upright in his prime, and uses a cane in old age"— earned him a kingdom and everlasting fame.

Chances are you won't make history by solving the riddles in this book, but you may just find yourself having a lot of fun. Read them with a friend and see who groans first. Here's one for starters: What does an orange do when placed on a table?

Give up? The answer's inside.

What does an orange do
when placed on the
breakfast table?

It looks

round.

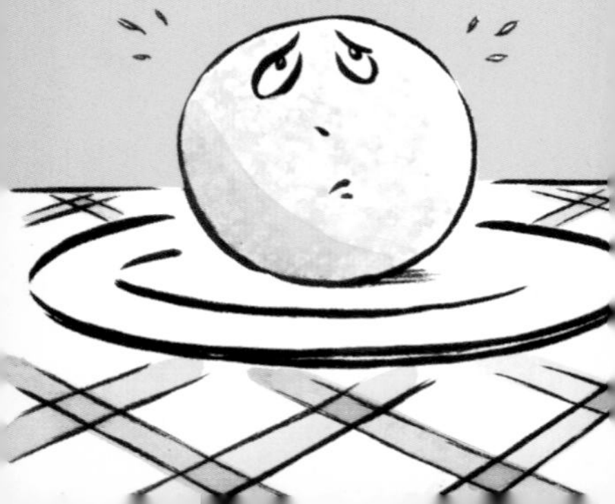

What most resembles half a
watermelon?

The other **half**

Their trunks are all packed
and they wave their
salutes.
Will they hurry away on
the wing?
Don't worry, my dear;
you'll not lose them.
Don't fear!
They never do leave 'till
the spring.

When is it easy to read
in the woods?

Ha Hee Ha

Hee Ho Hee

Hee

When autumn
turns the
leaves

Ho Hee Ha He

Ho Ho

Hee Ha

What animal changes size twice a day?

A **cat**, which is let out at night and taken in in the morning

What is purchased by the yard and worn by the foot?

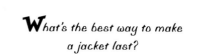

What's the best way to make
a jacket last?

Make the
pants and vest
first.

Some have two eyes,
 some have four;
You can buy them at the store.
Some are white, or black, or red:
Their lives oft hang just
 by a thread.

Buttons

What's the difference
between one yard and
two yards?

Ho

Ha

Har

Hee

Ho

Hee

Ho

Ha

Usually a **fence**

Har

Hee

Ha

Ha

How is a centipede one of
the tallest living creatures?

It stands over

one hundred feet.

What animal would you like
to be on a cold day?

A little 'otter

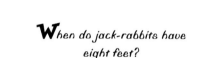

When do jack-rabbits have eight feet?

When there are

two of them!

Why is a caterpillar such an upright creature?

He's always
turning over a
new leaf.

Why does the ocean

get angry?

Because it's

crossed

so often

Does it fear the sun, or why
Does it behave so very shy?
It always right behind me goes
When sunshine falls upon
     my nose.
'Tis mine, as any one can see;
It looks, sometimes, so
     much like me!

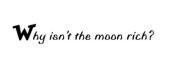

Why isn't the moon rich?

Because it spends its

quarters

getting full

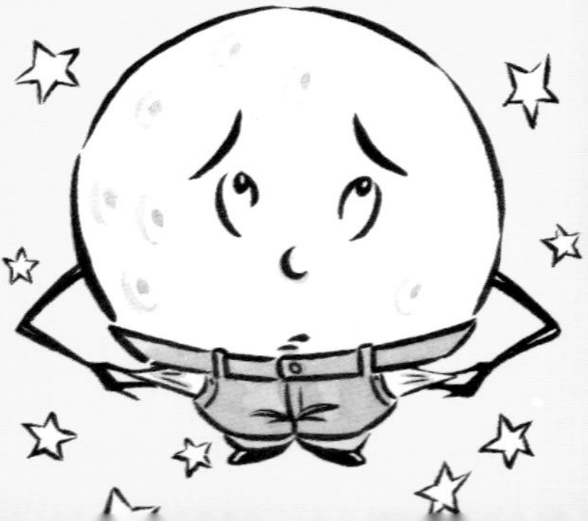

I went out walking one day and met three panhandlers. To the first I gave ten cents, to the second I also gave ten cents, and to the third I gave but five—what time of day was it?

Ho

Ha

Har

Hee

Ho

Hee

Hee

e

Ha

Ho

Ho

Ha

A quarter to

three

Har

Hee

H

Ha

Ha

Har

Ha

Ho

What's a waist of time?

the middle of an

hourglass

They are pretty and polished,
But each one demands
A quite close inspection
Of faces and hands.
Yet you never need worry;
Their features will pass
A most careful inspection;
They're kept under glass.

Watches

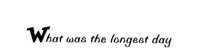

What was the longest day
of Adam's life?

The one on which
there was no

Eve

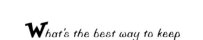

What's the best way to keep
someone's love?

When it is a good thing to
lose your temper?

What's the largest room
in the world?

Har

Ha

Ho

Ha

Har

Ho

Hee

The room for

improvement

Ha

Ha

Ho

Har

Ho

Hee

Har

Har

Ho

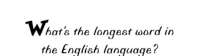

What's the longest word in the English language?

Smiles,

ONE MILE

because there's a mile between the first and last letter.

How may book-keeping be taught in a lesson of three words?

Never **lend** them.

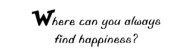

Where can you always
find happiness?

What is it that, after you take away the whole, some still remains?

Wholesome

What is at the beginning
of eternity,
The end of time and space,
The beginning of
every end,
And the end of every race?

Ho Ha Har Ho Hee Ho Hee Ha Hee

The letter
"E"

Ha Hee Har Ha Ha

*H*ow many apples were
eaten in the Garden of Eden?

Ten:

*Eve ate,
Adam too*

Who was the fastest runner
in the world?

Adam—

he was first in
the human race.

Why didn't the ancients use slates and pencils?

Because the Lord told them
to multiply on the
face of the **earth**.

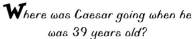

Where was Caesar going when he was 39 years old?

A boy is on a train, which is moving at the rate of 50 miles an hour. He jumps up three feet. Where does he land?

In the
same place
from which he jumped

A parade comes down the street. An elephant walks in front of two elephants; an elephant walks behind two elephants; and an elephant walks between two elephants. How many elephants are in the parade?

Three

When is a woman
duplicated?

When she's

beside

herself

When is a man obliged
to keep his word?

When no one will

take it

What is that which is often
brought to table and cut,
but never eaten?

A pack of
cards

What's the difference
between a gardener and a
billiard player?

Ho Ha Har
Hee
Ho
e
Ho

One minds his
peas,
the other his
cues.

Ha

Ha

Har
Ha
Hee

Ha
a Har
Ha

Why is it dangerous for farmers to plant peas during a war?

The enemy might come along and **shell them**.

What's strange about
flowers?

They shoot
before they have
pistils.

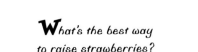

What's the best way
to raise strawberries?

We are little airy
      creatures,
All of different voice
      and features.
One of us in glass is set;
One of us you'll find in jet;
One of us is set in tin;
And the fourth a box
      within;
If the last you should
      pursue,
It can never fly from you.

The vowels:

a, e, i, o, u

Does any word contain
all the vowels?

Unquestion-
ably!

Why is a room full of married folks like an empty room?

Ho

Ha

Har

Ho

Hee   Hee   Ha

Because there's not a

single person

in it

Ha

Har

Hee

Har

Ha

Why is an empty purse
so monotonous?

What's the difference
between an old penny and
a new dime?

When can you carry water
in a sieve?

Ho

Ha

Har

Ho

Hee

Hee

Ho

Hee

When the water's

frozen

Har

Ha

Hee

Hee

Ha

Har

Ha

Ha

What asks no questions, but
requires many answers?

The
doorbell

In a certain family one of the boys stated that he had twice as many sisters as brothers. One of his sisters replied, "Well, that's funny, because I have just as many sisters as brothers." How many boys and girls were there in the family?

The boy had two brothers
and four sisters;
the girl had three brothers
and three sisters.
Thus, there were three
boys and four girls
in the family.

If your uncle's sister is not
your aunt, what relation
is she to you?

Why are the Western prairies flat?

Because the sun

sets on them

every night.

There's a man who works in a candy store in Boston who is 6 feet 6 inches high, has a waist measure of 42 inches and wears a size 12 shoe. What do you think he weighs?

He weighs
candy!

My sweetheart gave me one.
Where is it now?
I had it. It has gone—
I don't know how.

And yet, it seems to me,
I liked it very well.
Here, there, where can it be?
'Twas on my lips to tell.

Ha Hee Hee

Hee Hee Ho

Hee

Har

A kiss

Hee

Ha Har Hee

Ho Ho

Hee Ho

Hee Har

What do we often catch
yet never see?

A **passing**
remark

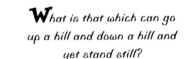

What is that which can go up a hill and down a hill and yet stand still?

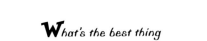

What's the best thing
to part with?

How many balls of string
would it take to reach
the sun?

Only one—
if it's long enough!

This book has been bound using handcraft methods, and Smyth-sewn to ensure durability.

The dust jacket was designed by E. June Roberts and illustrated by Rollin McGrail. The interior was designed by Paul Kepple. The interior was illustrated by Rollin McGrail. The text was edited by Melissa Stein. The text was set in Improv and Biffo by Deborah Lugar.